WALKING BY FAITH

A Study of How Faith Works in Our Daily Lives

by Heath Rogers

2019 One Stone Press.
All rights reserved. No part of this book may be reproduced
in any form without written permission of the publisher.

Published by:
One Stone Press
979 Lovers Lane
Bowling Green, KY 42103

Printed in the United States of America

ISBN 13: 978-1-941422-43-4

1-800-428-0121
www.onestone.com

CONTENTS

Lesson 1	Noah - A Faith That Stands Out To God	7
Lesson 2	Abraham - A Faith That Passes the Test	15
Lesson 3	Joseph - A Faith That Overcomes the Challenges of Life	23
Lesson 4	Joshua and Caleb – Faith In God's Promise	31
Lesson 5	Hannah - A Faith That Remains Faithful	39
Lesson 6	David - Faith To Face A Giant	47
Lesson 7	Josiah - A Faith That Overcomes Poor Role Models	55
Lesson 8	Shadrach, Meshach, & Abednego - Faith in the Face of Fire	61
Lesson 9	Nehemiah - The Faith To Build	67
Lesson 10	Esther - A Courageous Faith	75
Lesson 11	Peter - A Faith That Walks On Water	83
Lesson 12	Martha & Mary - Making Priorities A Matter of Faith	89
Lesson 13	Jesus - A Faith That Gets Us Through A Crisis	97

Introduction

"Now faith is the substance of things hoped for, the evidence of things not seen" (Heb. 11:1).

We know that faith plays an important part in one becoming a Christian. We must hear, believe, repent, confess and be baptized. However, the Scriptures clearly teach that faith must play a role in our entire life as a Christian.

The apostle Paul wrote, "For we walk by faith, not by sight" (2 Cor. 5:7). In the New Testament, the word "walk" is often used to refer to the way we live our daily life. One of the greatest challenges for the Christian is learning how to live in the presence of spiritual realities he cannot see, while being surrounded by a physical world given over to sin, error and unbelief. It is a great challenge, but it can be done.

The lessons in this workbook are character studies of men and women who show us how to "walk by faith." Many of these people were called upon to face challenges much greater than we will ever face, but they overcame these challenges through their faith. From their example we will learn the role faith is to play in our daily lives; that is - we will learn how to "walk by faith."

I am especially grateful to Mark Anspach for taking the time to proofread this material. Many of the suggestions he made have become a part of this workbook.

Unless otherwise noted, all Bible quotations are taken from the New King James Version.

Lesson 1

NOAH
A Faith That Stands Out To God

Faith Causes One To Stand Out To God

People may think we live in troubling times. Violence is on the rise while morality is on the decline. However, Noah lived in a world that was much more wicked than our own time. "Then the Lord saw that the wickedness of man was great in the earth, and that every intent of the thoughts of his heart was only evil continually" (Gen. 6:5). The earth was given over to corruption and violence (vv. 12-13). In fact, the people had become so wicked God was sorry He had made man (vv. 6-7).

However, in this mass of evil, corruption, wickedness, and violence—Noah stood out to the Lord. He found grace in the eyes of the Lord (v. 8) and was the one bright spot in an otherwise dark and depraved world.

Noah's example tells us that we can also stand out to the Lord. It pays to be a righteous young man or woman of faith. No one around us may seem to notice or care—but God does!

> Noah lived in a world that was much more wicked than our own time.

1. Describe the world in which Noah lived (include the verses with your answer). _____
   _____
   _____

2. Make a list of how the world in which we live is better/worse than that of Noah's time. _____
   _____
   _____

3. Why do you think Noah found grace in the eyes of the Lord? Why do you think he stood out? _____
   _____

4. What promise is found in Psalm 34:15? _____
   _____

Faith Is A Belief In Things Not Seen

Noah was a man of faith. "By faith Noah, being divinely warned of things not yet seen, moved with godly fear, prepared an ark for the saving of his household, by which he condemned the world and became heir of the righteousness which is according to faith" (Heb. 11:7).

The Bible defines faith in Hebrews 11:1. "Now faith is the substance of things hoped for, the evidence of things not seen." Notice that Noah was "divinely warned of things not yet seen." Noah was told the world was going to be destroyed by water (Gen. 6:13, 17). There had never been an episode of world-wide destruction before, but Noah believed the world was going to be destroyed by a great flood because he believed God.

Paul said Christians "walk by faith, not by sight" (2 Cor. 5:7). Our lives are guided, not so much by physical realities we witness with our physical eyes, but by spiritual realities we see with our eyes of faith. We can "see" God in Heaven and Jesus sitting on His right hand reigning as King. We can "see" a divine standard of right and wrong. We can "see" there is an eternal Heaven and Hell. We live by faith in God and His word, believing it because He said it. Romans 10:17—"So then _____ comes by _____, and _____ by the _____ of God."

5. Discuss some challenges Noah had to overcome in order to believe God would destroy the world with water. _____
_____
_____

6. What is faith? In your own words, explain what Hebrews 11:1 means. _____
_____
_____
_____

7. From where does faith come (Rom. 10:17)? _____
_____

8. How do you grow in your faith? _____
_____
_____

9. What does it mean to "walk by faith"? _____
_____
_____

Faith Is Known By Its Actions

By faith Noah obeyed God. He prepared an ark for the salvation of his household (Heb. 11:7). Noah believed what God said about the coming destruction of the world. He built the ark because God had told him he would be kept alive in it (Gen. 6:17-19). Had Noah not built the ark he would not have been saved.

There is no doubt that we are saved by faith, but the faith that saves us is a faith that obeys God's will. James 2:14-26 discusses the proper relationship between faith and works of obedience. James begins by asking the question, "What does it profit, my brethren, if someone says he has faith but does not have works? Can faith save him?" (v. 14). He goes on in the remaining verses to show how faith without works cannot save us. If we are saved today, we must express our faith in works of obedience to the word of God.

The Size Of The Ark

The ark was 300 cubits long or 450 feet. A football field is 100 yards long or 300 feet. The ark is 150 feet longer than a football field. The ark was 50 cubits wide or 75 feet. A football field is 53.3 yards wide or 160 feet.

The Ark

·10 ·20 ·30 ·40 50 40· 30· 20· 10·

10. What would have happened to Noah had he not built the ark? _____

11. Faith without works is _____ (James 2:17, 26). What does this mean? How does it apply to us today? _____

12. Abraham was justified by _____ (James 2:21).

13. Can one be saved by "faith only" today (James 2:24)? Explain your answer. __

Faith Requires Attention To Detail

Noah did not just build a boat. God gave Noah the exact pattern for the ark (Gen. 6:14-16).

- The materials for the ark consisted of gopher wood, and it was to be covered inside and outside with pitch.
- The ark was to be exactly 300 cubits long, 50 cubits wide and 30 cubits high. A cubit is about 18 inches, which means the ark was 450 x 75 x 45 feet.
- The ark was to have one window and one door.
- The ark was to be made with three decks and was to be filled with rooms.

Genesis 6:22—"Thus Noah did; according to _____ that God commanded, so he did."

While there are religious minded people today who tend to ignore the details of God's word, those who walk by faith know better. One who has true faith in God will pay attention to the details. God has given a divine pattern for marriage and the home, how to live godly lives, how the church is to work and worship God, and how one is to become a Christian. Heaven is for those who do God's will. Matthew 7:21—"Not everyone who says to Me, '_____, _____,' shall _____ the kingdom of heaven, but he who _____ the _____ of My Father in heaven." Explain this verse in your own words. _____

_____

_____

14. What do you think would have happened to the ark if Noah had not followed God's complete instructions in detail? Do you think it would have survived the flood? _____

_____

15. What was Jesus' attitude towards the details of God's law (Matt. 5:18-19)? __

_____

_____

16. Are you obedient to your parents if you add to or delete from their instructions? Explain your answer. _____
_____
_____
_____

17. Are you obedient to God if you add to or delete from His instructions? Explain your answer. _____
_____
_____

18. Identify some areas of your life today where God has provided a pattern to be followed. _____
_____
_____

Faith Is Rewarded

By faith Noah was moved to prepare an ark for the saving of his household (Heb. 11:7). Because Noah believed in God's warning and followed God's directions, he and those with him on the ark survived the destruction of the flood.

The same thing is true for us today. If we will trust in the Lord and obey His will, we will receive Heaven as our eternal home (1 Pet. 1:3-5).

19. How was Noah's faith rewarded (Gen. 6:22; Heb. 11:7)? _____
_____
_____

20. How will our faith be rewarded? _____
_____
_____

Conclusion

Noah was a man of great faith in an otherwise faithless world. His faith is a great and encouraging example to all of us today. From Noah we learn that faith is the result of our trust in God, that faith must be expressed in works of obedience, and that the details are important to God. One day our faith will be rewarded because it pleases God and makes us "stand out" to God.

Lesson 2

ABRAHAM
A Faith That Passes The Test

Abraham was a man of great faith. Like anything else, in order to be great, one's faith must be tried and strengthened. We know Abraham's faith was great because it passed a great test.

When Abraham was 75 years old, God called him to leave his father's home and travel to a land which He would give his descendants after him (Gen. 12:1-9). The strange thing about this promise was that Abraham had no children. He talked with God about this matter, and God assured him that a child would come from his own body and his descendants would eventually be more numerous than the stars of heaven. Although this seemed impossible, Abraham believed God's promise (Gen. 15:4-6; Rom. 4:18-22).

> Abraham's faith was great because it passed a great test.

Abraham waited an additional 25 years before this child was born. Think for a moment what it must have been like for Abraham, already advanced in age, to wait 25 more years to have a child? Do you think it was difficult for Abraham to wait this long? _____ Have you ever waited a long time for something? _____
How did you feel about waiting? _____
_____

Why do you think waiting for something is difficult? ___
_____
_____

God had promised Abraham a child, and the child finally came. Then God commanded Abraham to do something that seemed impossible: "Now it came to pass after these things that God tested Abraham, and said to him, 'Abraham!' And he said, 'Here I am.' Then He said, 'Take now your son, your only son Isaac, whom you love, and go to the land of Moriah, and offer him there as a burnt offering on one of the mountains of which I shall tell you'" (Gen. 22:1-2).

This was indeed a great test for Abraham. He waited 25 years for God to give him a son so his descendants would become more numerous than the stars of heaven. Now that he has received this son, God tells Abraham to kill him! This doesn't make sense. There is an obvious conflict between God's promise and God's command. The way Abraham reacted to this command provides a great lesson for our own faith today.

1. What did God call Abraham (Isaiah 41:8)? _____

2. Why do you think God called him this? Consider John 15:14 in your answer.
   _____
   _____

3. Explain why God's command to offer Isaac was such a great test to Abraham's faith? What was the conflict between God's promise and God's command? __
   _____
   _____
   _____

Abraham Was Quick To Obey

Abraham reacted to this puzzling command in a surprising manner: he promptly obeyed (Gen. 22:3). Abraham did not turn his back on God. He could have said, "No, I will not sacrifice my son, whom I love, for anything, including You," but he didn't. Abraham could have taken time to ponder the commandment and try to make sense of it. He could have reasoned, "As soon as I can understand why God has asked this of me, I will go," but he didn't. Abraham "rose early in the morning" and departed in obedience to God's command (v. 3).

It was sometime during the three-day journey to the mountain that Abraham had reconciled the inconsistency between God's promise and God's command. He had come to the conclusion that God would raise Isaac from the dead (Heb. 11:17-19). Notice, before ascending the mountain to make the sacrifice, Abraham told his two servants, "Stay here with the donkey; the lad and I will go yonder and worship, and *we* will come back to you" (Gen. 22:5, emphasis mine, HR). Abraham may not have understood exactly how it was possible, but he believed Isaac would come back with him.

There are commandments in God's word that some people do not understand. "Why do I have to be baptized?" "Why do I have to become a member of the church?" "Why can't I do this or that?" Those who have a strong faith in God do not have to understand the reasons behind God's commands before they obey. They will simply obey what God has told them to do.

4. How did Abraham react to God's command (Gen. 22:3)? _____

_____

_____

5. Did Abraham have to understand the reason or purpose for God's command before he would obey? Explain. _____

_____

_____

6. What did Abraham believe God would do to Isaac (Heb. 11:17-19)? _____

_____

_____

7. Is there a command God has given you that you question or don't understand? What is it? _____

_____

_____

Abraham Had Shared His Faith

Abraham is considered the father of the Jews (Matt. 3:9). The reason Abraham was made the father of God's people was because he would be a good father and teach his children about the Lord (Gen. 18:19). This is exactly what Abraham did. Notice the question his son Isaac asked as they were traveling up the mountain to make the sacrifice unto God: "Look, the fire and the wood, but where is the lamb for a burnt offering?" (Gen. 22:7). Isaac had seen his father offer enough sacrifices to know there was supposed to be a lamb. Something was missing. Abraham had taught his son well.

People of faith seek to share their faith with others. Doing so will accomplish at least two things. First, it will help others to be saved. Second, sharing our faith will help strengthen our faith. Sharing our faith requires us to study and know the word of God well enough to understand it, defend it, and teach it (2 Tim. 2:15; 1 Pet. 3:15).

- "Be _____ to present yourself _____ to God, a worker who does not need to be _____, rightly _____ the word of truth" (2 Tim. 2:15).

- "But sanctify the Lord God in your hearts, and _____ be _____ to give a _____ to everyone who asks you a _____ for the hope that is in you, with meekness and fear" (1 Peter 3:15).

Abraham Put God First

When they came to the place chosen by God, Abraham built an altar, put his son upon the altar, and took hold of the knife to kill his son. At that moment, the Angel of the Lord cried out to stop Abraham. He said, "Do not lay your hand on the lad, or do anything to him; for now I know that you fear God, since you have not withheld your son, your only son, from Me" (Gen. 22:12).

Abraham passed the test. He proved to himself and to God that he would not put anything before God, not even his only son whom he loved.

8. List some things a person might put before God. _____
   _____
   _____
   _____

This command of God tested Abraham in a couple ways. First, it tested Abraham's willingness to obey God even when God didn't seem to make sense. How was God going to bless Abraham with descendants through Isaac if Isaac died? Second, it tested Abraham's loyalty to God. The fact that Abraham was willing to give his son to God meant he would be willing to give anything to God—God came first with Abraham.

The Lord requires the same thing from us today. Jesus said, "He who loves father or mother more than Me is not worthy of Me. And he who loves son or daughter more than Me is not worthy of Me" (Matt. 10:37).

9. List some ways you have seen Chrisitans put their family members before their service to God. _____
   _____
   _____

10. What did God have to say about Abraham's parenting skills (Gen. 18:19)? __
    _____
    _____

11. Explain how sharing our faith (teaching others the gospel, defending what we believe, etc.) will help to strengthen our faith. _____
    _____
    _____

12. Explain the requirements for becoming a Christian, and provide Bible verses to support these requirements. _____
    _____
    _____
    _____

13. What did Abraham prove when he was willing to sacrifice his own son at God's command? _____
_____
_____

14. Who must come first in our life (Matt. 10:37)? _____
_____
_____

Abraham's Faith Was Rewarded

The Bible teaches that one's faith in God will be rewarded (Heb. 11:6). This is certainly the case with Abraham. Listen to what Abraham was told after he passed this test:

> "¹⁵ Then the Angel of the Lord called to Abraham a second time out of heaven, ¹⁶ and said: 'By Myself I have sworn, says the Lord, because you have done this thing, and have not withheld your son, your only son — ¹⁷ blessing I will bless you, and multiplying I will multiply your descendants as the stars of the heaven and as the sand which is on the seashore; and your descendants shall possess the gate of their enemies. ¹⁸ In your seed all the nations of the earth shall be blessed, because you have obeyed My voice'" (Gen. 22:15-18)

Our faith will be rewarded as well. Our descendants may not become a great nation, and we may not inherit a land of our own, but we will receive the salvation of our souls. "Whom having not seen you love. Though now you do not see Him, yet believing, you rejoice with joy inexpressible and full of glory, receiving the end of your faith - the salvation of your souls" (1 Pet. 1:8-9).

15. "But without _____ it is impossible to _____ Him, for he who comes to God must _____ that He is, and that He is a _____ of those who diligently _____ Him" (Heb. 11:6).

16. Describe the blessing Abraham received from God because of his obedience (Gen. 22:15-18). _____
   _____
   _____

17. What is the ultimate reward we will receive for our faith? _____
   _____
   _____

Conclusion

Abraham was a man of great faith. His faith withstood the test of time: he waited 25 years for a promise from God; the test of reason: God's command appeared to be in contrast with His promise; the test of loyalty: Abraham put God before everyone – including his only son.

Our faith will be tested numerous times in this life. It is during these times that we, like Abraham, must fully rely upon God.

JOSEPH
A Faith That Overcomes The Challenges Of Life

Jacob had twelve sons, but Joseph was his favorite. He showed preference to Joseph by giving him a special coat (Gen. 37:3-4). Joseph's brothers reacted to this situation by hating Joseph. They refused to speak kindly or peaceably with him. To make matters worse, Joseph had dreams in which he was elevated above his father and his older brothers (vv. 5-11). His brothers envied him and hated him even more. Have there ever been times when your siblings, classmates or peers have been shown favoritism? _____ How do you feel when this happens? _____
_____
_____

One day Jacob sent Joseph to see how his brothers were doing. The brothers saw Joseph coming towards them and plotted to get rid of him. Originally they planned to kill Joseph, but instead they sold him to Midianite traders who took him down to Egypt and sold him into slavery (vv. 23-28).

As a young man, Joseph was called upon to suffer a number of challenges unfairly. Although his situation was extreme, the challenges he faced are very common. Let's consider the example of Joseph and learn how a young person can use his faith to overcome the challenges of life.

> Joseph was called upon to suffer a number of challenges unfairly.

The Challenge Of Bitterness

From the beginning, Joseph was faced with the challenge of not becoming bitter. Bitterness is a strong feeling of hatred, resentment or cynicism. Bitterness is also described as anger "gone to seed" or unresolved anger. That is, bitterness is what happens when we bury our anger and allow it to grow, becoming worse and worse. Think about Joseph's situation for a moment. He went from being the favorite son to being a slave—someone's property. He could not help the fact that his father treated him differently than his brothers. It was not his fault, but he bore the brunt of their resentment.

However, this was not the only time Joseph would be called upon to suffer as an innocent man. His master's wife falsely accused him of trying to assault her and he was cast into prison (Gen. 39:7-20). Then, he was forgotten by the chief butler and left in prison (Gen. 40:14-15, 23). Any of these circumstances would cause one to become bitter, but Joseph resisted every urge to allow anger and bitterness to remain in his heart.

1. In your own words, describe what bitterness is. _____
   _____
   _____

2. Why is bitterness such a bad thing? _____
   _____
   _____

3. What are we to do with bitterness (Eph. 4:31)? _____
   _____
   _____

4. How can our faith help us overcome the temptation to become bitter? ____
   _____
   _____

5. Recall a situation or event that caused you to feel bitter. How did you overcome this feeling? _____

_____

_____

The Challenge Of Lust

Joseph was around seventeen years old when he was sold as a slave to Potiphar. He was a handsome and productive servant (Gen. 39:1-6). He caught the eye of his master's wife who made advances upon him (v. 7).

Joseph could have said, "yes." He could have used any number of arguments to justify his actions. However, he refused. He told his master's wife, "How then can I do this great wickedness and sin against God?" (vv. 8-9). Joseph rejected this invitation because he rightfully understood it to be a sin against God.

On another occasion, his master's wife grabbed Joseph by his clothes and told him to lie with her. He left his garments in her hand and fled outside (v. 12). The New Testament tells us to "Flee fornication!" (1 Cor. 6:18), and that is exactly what Joseph did.

6. Think about it: what are some arguments Joseph could have used to justify lying with his master's wife? _____

_____

_____

7. What did Joseph say about the sin of fornication? In particular, who was it a sin against (Gen. 39:9)? _____

_____

_____

8. What are some things that a young man or young woman may do or say to entice the opposite sex? Are such things fitting for a person who is walking by faith? _____
_____
_____
_____
_____

9. What action are we to take in regards to sexual sins (1 Cor. 6:18)? _____
_____
_____
_____

> What are some challenges you may face or have seen your friends face?

The Challenge Of Despair

People can make it through almost anything as long as they have hope. However, when hope is lost, it seems that all is lost.

Joseph had very little to hope for.

- He was sold into slavery and taken away from his home. He had no hope of his family rescuing him because it was his family (his brothers) who had sold him into slavery.
- He did the right thing by refusing the advances of his master's wife, but he went to prison anyway.
- In prison he was forgotten by Pharaoh's butler.

A person can only take so much. It would have been easy for Joseph to have lost hope during any of these situations, but he didn't. His example teaches us that no matter what comes our way, there is no reason to abandon our hope or our faith in God.

10. How can suffering cause one to despair? _____
_____
_____

11. Hebrews 6:19 describes our hope as the anchor of our soul. Describe how our hope works as an anchor for our soul? _____
_____
_____

12. Have you ever felt hopeless or wanted to give up? How did you get back your feeling of hope? _____
_____
_____

The Challenge Of Pride

Pharaoh had a dream and Joseph was brought from prison to interpret this dream (Gen. 41). Joseph informed Pharaoh that a severe famine was coming and then told him how to prepare for it. Pharaoh rewarded Joseph by promoting him to the second most powerful man in Egypt (vv. 38-44).

Think about this: Joseph went from being an imprisoned slave to the second most powerful person in the entire nation—overnight! This provided a great temptation for one to become proud and arrogant, but Joseph passed this test.

Pride is dangerous because it causes us to forget about God and elevate ourselves above God. Joseph overcame pride by remembering God had made all of this possible (Gen. 41:15-16). Even Pharaoh acknowledged that God had worked through Joseph (vv. 38-39). Likewise, we can overcome the challenge of pride by humbling ourselves in the sight of the Lord (James 4:6, 10).

13. What happened in Joseph's life that could have caused him to be tempted by pride? _____
_____
_____

14. Why is pride dangerous? _____
_____
_____

15. "_____ goes before _____, and a _____ spirit before a _____" (Prov. 16:18).

16. How did Joseph overcome pride (Gen. 41:15-16)? _____
_____
_____

17. Has pride ever entered you heart because of your abilities or accomplishments? How did you handle this challenge? _____
_____
_____

The Challenge Of Vengeance

As time went on, the seven years of drought eventually affected Joseph's family. They heard there was grain in Egypt, and Jacob sent his sons there to buy grain. They were brought before Joseph, but they did not recognize him as their brother (Gen. 42:1-9).

By many people's standards, Joseph would have had every right to seek vengeance upon his brothers. It was their fault that he suffered so much as a slave in Egypt. He had power over them and could have easily had them executed. However, he did not seek vengeance upon them.

He eventually revealed himself to them (Gen. 45:3-8). When he did so, his brothers were dismayed and grieved. They knew he had every right to hate them and punish them for what they had done to him. However, Joseph reassured them that he would not harm them. He had no hatred for them.

How was Joseph able to overcome the challenge of vengeance? Joseph had a strong faith and saw God's hand in everything that had happened. Take special note of the things Joseph said about God to his brothers:

- "for God sent me before you to preserve life" (v. 5).
- "And God sent me before you to preserve a posterity for you in the earth, and to save your lives by a great deliverance" (v. 7).
- "So now it was not you who sent me here, but God" (v. 8).

Through faith, Joseph was able to see he had no cause to be angry. His being sold into Egypt was God's way of providing for his family.

Terrible things may happen to us in our life, but we are not allowed to seek vengeance. God will right all the wrongs that need to be corrected. "Beloved, do not _____ yourselves, but rather give place to _____; for it is written, '_____ is Mine, I will _____,' says the Lord" (Rom. 12:19).

18. What are some arguments Joseph could have used to justify taking vengeance upon his brothers? _____

19. How did Joseph view his being sold into slavery (Gen. 45:5-8)? _____

20. To whom does vengeance belong (Rom. 12:19)? _____

Conclusion

If ever a young man had a good argument to abandon his faith, it would have been Joseph. He was called upon to face extreme challenges regarding bitterness, lust, despair, pride, and vengeance. He faced and overcame all of these challenges through his faith.

We may not be called upon to face such extreme challenges, but we will face challenges in our life. We will have to stand up to peer-pressure. We will have to say "no" to opportunities to try drugs, alcohol and tobacco, to engage in sexual immorality, and to be rebellious to authority. Our beliefs will be challenged by the false doctrines and empty philosophies that abound in our world. Let us strengthen our faith now so it will help us through these challenges when they do come upon us.

JOSHUA AND CALEB
Faith In God's Promise

After leaving Egypt and receiving the Law at Mount Sinai, Moses brought the children of Israel to the border of the Promised Land. Twelve men (one man from each tribe) were sent to spy out the land. The men spent forty days traveling throughout the land.

They brought back a unanimous report (Num. 13:26-29). The land was fruitful, "it flows with milk and honey." And the land was occupied with strong giants and fortified cities.

However, there was a difference among the spies with regard to Israel's ability to take the land. Caleb said, "We are well able to overcome" (v. 30). Joshua appears to have agreed with this report (14:6-10). The other spies said, "We are not able to go up against the people" (v. 31).

Joshua and Caleb came from the same nation as the other ten spies. They had the same background and were of the same religion. They went into the same territory and saw the same things. What made Joshua and Caleb's conclusion so different than that of the other ten spies? The answer lies in their faith.

> **What made Joshua and Caleb different from the other ten spies? The answer lies in their faith.**

They Walked By Faith, Not By Sight

God's people are to walk by faith, not by sight (2 Cor. 5:7). The contrast between the ten spies and Joshua and Caleb gives us a great example of what it means to walk by faith.

1. The ten spies were walking by sight. They saw obstacles:
   - They said the people of Canaan were stronger (Num. 13:31).
   - They saw a land that devoured its inhabitants, defeating those who tried to attack them.
   - They were already defeated. They said they would fall by the sword and their wives and children would become victims (14:3).
2. Joshua and Caleb were walking by faith. They saw victory:
   - They saw no need for delay. "Let us go up at once and take possession, for we are well able to overcome it" (13:30).
   - They saw God's hand in this matter (14:8). They did not have to be bigger or stronger than the people of the land. God was in control of the situation and He would give them the land.
   - They knew the protection of the people of Canaan was gone. "The Lord is with us" (14:9).

There will be times when we will face incredible obstacles in our lives. If we are walking by sight, we will see defeat. However, if we walk with a strong faith in God, we will see opportunity and victory. It really does depend on how we choose to look at these situations.

1. "For we walk by _____, not by _____" (2 Cor. 5:7).

2. Describe the obstacles mentioned by the ten spies (Num. 13:31-33). _____
   _____
   _____
   _____

3. What did they believe would happen to them and their families (Num. 14:3)?
   _____
   _____

4. Why were Joshua and Caleb so confident in their ability to take the land (Num. 14:8-9)? _____

_____

_____

5. Have you ever doubted God's ability to help you overcome an obstacle or challenge in your life? Give an example. _____

_____

_____

They Trusted In God's Promise

God had promised to give them this land. "Send men to spy out the land of Canaan, which I am giving to the children of Israel..." (Num. 13:2). In fact, this was a promise that went all the way back to their fathers (Deut. 6:23). The promise was given to Abraham (Gen. 12:7, 13:14-15). The promise was repeated to Jacob (Gen. 28:13). The promise was repeated to Moses (Ex. 3:8, 17). This promise was very much a part of their heritage, and it should have been a part of their faith.

Joshua and Caleb believed this promise. Believing that God keeps His word and gives us the blessings He has promised is an important part of our faith. "But without faith it is impossible to please Him, for he who comes to God must believe that He is, and that *He is a rewarder of those who diligently seek Him*" (Heb. 11:6; emphasis mine - HR). We must believe that God will do what He says He will do. We cannot please God if we doubt His promises.

A lack of faith gives way to doubt, fear, and complaints. All of these negative qualities are expressed by the Israelites in this incident. Having faith in God means we believe in His promises; we believe God keeps His word.

They Trusted In God's Power

Anyone can make a promise, but Joshua and Caleb knew God had the power to keep His promise.

God had already kept one of His promises to Abraham. He promised to make a great nation out of an old man with no children. If God could bring life out of a "dead" body (see Romans 4:18-21), then He could surely give Israel a land already occupied by a strong people.

God had proven His great power to Israel when He delivered them from Egypt and sustained them in the wilderness (Num. 14:22). They had absolutely no reason to doubt God's ability.

Likewise, we must remember the power of God. He is able to give us everything we need in this life, both physically and spiritually (Eph. 1:17-19).

"And my _____ shall supply _____ your _____ according to His _____ in glory by Christ Jesus" (Phil. 4:19).

6. What promise had God made to Abraham regarding the land of Canaan (Gen. 12:7; 17:8)? _____
_____
_____

7. Thought Question: Can we really say that we have faith in God if we do not trust Him to keep His promises? Why or why not? Consider Hebrews 11:6 in your answer. _____
_____
_____

8. What promise to Abraham had God already fulfilled (Gen. 12:2; Ex. 1:7)? ___
_____
_____
_____

9. How had God shown His power to the Children of Israel (Num. 14:22)? ___
_____
_____
_____

10. Do you keep promises you have made? How do you feel when others break their promises to you? _____
   _____
   _____
   _____

They Weren't Afraid To Stand Against Their Brethren

It takes great courage to stand against our enemies, but even greater courage to stand against our friends.

The ten spies brought back a bad report (The King James Version calls it an "evil report" - Num. 13:32). Joshua and Caleb had a different take on the situation. They agreed the land was good. They did not deny it was filled with strong cities and occupied by strong people. However, they said "we are able to overcome" them and take possession.

On the following day they found themselves in opposition to more than the other ten spies. The entire nation was rejecting their good report (Num. 14:1-10). They tried to get the Israelites to understand that God would fulfill His promise and give them the land. They told them there was no reason to fear the people of Canaan and that they were actually rebelling against God by refusing to go in and take the land (v. 9). The people were ready to stone them to death because of these words. In rejecting Joshua and Caleb's warning, they were turning on the ones who were trying to help them do the right thing.

We know there are enemies who are "without." The people of the world will always resist and reject the truth of God's word (John 15:18-19; 2 Tim. 3:13). Standing up for the Lord becomes even more difficult when we have to stand against our own friends and brethren. However, our faith must be so strong that our loyalty is given to God above all others.

They Were Of A Different Spirit

The faith of Joshua and Caleb caused them to stand out to God. He said that Caleb was of a "different spirit" than the rest of the people (Num. 14:24).
What do we know of Caleb's spirit?
- He *believed* the Lord. He expressed complete confidence in God's promises.
- He *heeded* the voice of the Lord (v. 22). He took God seriously.
- He *followed* the Lord *fully* (v. 24). He did everything God said to do.

The spirit of the people of Israel is detailed in Hebrews 3:16-19.
- They *rebelled*.
- They *sinned*.
- They *did not obey*.
- They were filled with *unbelief*.

What would God say of our spirit? Does He see us as faithful and obedient children who trust in Him, or as faithless, fearful people who rebel against Him?

11. What effect did the bad report of the ten spies have upon the children of Israel (Num. 14:1-4)? _____
   _____
   _____

12. What two things did Joshua and Caleb tell the people NOT to do (Num. 14:9)?
   _____
   _____
   _____

13. In your own words, explain why it would be more difficult to stand against your friends than to stand against your enemies. _____
   _____
   _____
   _____

14. Describe the difference between Joshua and Caleb (Num. 14:22-24) and the ten spies (Heb. 3:16-19). _____

    _____

    _____

    _____

15. Describe a situation where you had to stand against your friends. _____

    _____

    _____

    _____

Conclusion

God rewarded the faith of Joshua and Caleb on that day. He said they would live to enter into the land and gain their inheritance (Num. 14:24, 38). The ten spies who brought the bad report to Israel were killed by the Lord (vv. 36-37) and the people who believed their rebellious report died in the wilderness (vv. 32-35).

Our faith will be tested in this life. God's faithfulness gives us the hope we need to see past the trials of this life and focus upon the promise of Heaven. The writer of Hebrews encourages us to have the faith of Joshua and Caleb: to believe God's promise and obey His will so we can enter into our rest (Heb. 4:11).

Lesson 5

HANNAH
A Faith That Remains Faithful

The book of First Samuel records the lives of several important leaders in the history of Israel. However, the book begins with a brief account of a woman of great faith—Hannah, the mother of Samuel. We are introduced to her as a woman who is suffering under a great burden. Her faith helped her through this time of sorrow, but also kept her grounded as she experienced a time of great joy.

Hannah's Sorrows (1 Samuel 1:1-8)

Hannah's burden was actually caused by two things.

First, Hannah was barren. She could not have children because the Lord had closed her womb (v. 5). Barrenness was considered a great reproach upon a woman (Luke 1:25). The nation of Israel started out as a family and children were necessary for its perpetuation. Great emphasis was placed upon a man's heirs, thus a woman who could not give her husband male heirs felt as if she was letting down both her husband and her nation.

Second, Hannah was provoked by her rival (vv. 6-7). Her husband, Elkanah, had married a second wife named Peninnah. Peninnah would provoke Hannah in some manner because she could not have children. This made

> Hannah found herself in a very grave situation... She was suffering... Her faith helped her deal with the situation in the best possible way.

Hannah miserable. At a time of sacrifice and worship, when she should have been joyful, she "wept and did not eat" because of her sadness.

Hannah's husband did not help the situation, and he could not comfort her (v. 8). In fact, he actually added to Hannah's burden by his preference towards her (vv. 4-5) which likely caused Peninnah to hate her even more.

Hannah found herself in a very grave situation. She was suffering terribly through no fault of her own. However, her faith helped her deal with this situation in the best possible way. She did not return evil for evil. She did not lash out at her husband or Peninnah because of their behavior. She did not stop worshiping God. Instead, she took the matter to God in prayer.

1. What two things caused Hannah's sorrows? _____
   _____
   _____

2. Describe how Hannah's husband made things worse for her (vv. 4-5)? ____
   _____
   _____
   _____

3. Have you ever wanted something so much that it caused you sorrow when you did not receive it in a timely manner? What was it you desired? _____
   _____
   _____
   _____

Hannah' Prayer (1 Samuel 1:10-11)

Hannah went to the Tabernacle and, with great bitterness of her soul, she prayed to God and wept in anguish. Notice some important lessons to be learned from her prayer.

- She humbled herself before God. Hannah did not make demands of God. She identified herself as God's maidservant and asked that God not forget her. Strong faith in God allows us to combine two things which are often difficult to put together. Faith will give us confidence in prayer (James 1:5-6), and cause us to be humble before God (1 Pet. 5:5-6).

> **SAMUEL**
>
> Hannah named her son "Samuel," which means "heard of God." His very name was a reminder that God had heard and answered his mother's request. Samuel was living proof that God answers prayers.

- She made mention of her affliction. Hannah did the right thing when she asked God to look on her affliction. God cares about us and what we are experiencing. We are told to cast our cares upon God because He cares for us (1 Pet. 5:7; Phil. 4:6).

- She made a request of God. Hannah asked God to give her a male child. Like all prayer, this was a prayer of faith. Hannah knew God could grant this request because He had done so before. He had opened the womb of Sarah (Gen. 11:30, 18:14), Rebekah (Gen. 25:21), and Rachel (Gen. 29:31, 30:22). The Bible is filled with examples of God answering prayers. We know God delights in granting the requests of His children when they are offered according to His will (1 John 5:14-15).

- She made a vow. This request of Hannah's was different in that it included a vow. A vow is a promise or pledge to do a certain thing, or give certain things to God, in return for receiving certain blessings from God. Hannah's vow was simple. If God would grant her a male child, and thus take away her reproach, she would in turn give that child back to God.

Women of faith are not without problems in this life. The source of Hannah's problem was completely out of her control, so she took her problem to the One who was in control – God. We need to follow her example.

4. What attitude did Hannah have as she approached God in prayer (1 Pet. 5:5-6)? _____
_____

5. "Casting all your _____ upon Him, for He _____ for you" (1 Pet. 5:7).

6. Describe some ways we can cast our cares upon God. _____
_____
_____
_____

7. What promise is found in Philippians 4:6-7? _____
_____
_____
_____

8. What vow did Hannah make to God? _____
_____
_____

Hannah's Faithfulness (1 Samuel 1:19-28)

Sometimes people who are facing severe situations make impulsive promises to God failing to keep them once the situation has passed. Hannah had taken her troubles to the Lord, made her request for a male child, and even made a vow unto God. God answered Hannah's prayer (vv. 19-20). Now it was time for Hannah to make good on the promise she had made to God.

Hannah did not go to Shiloh to sacrifice with the family. Her plan was to stay home with her son until he was weaned. This would have taken three years. After that she would take him to Shiloh and leave him there to serve the Lord at the Tabernacle.

When the time came, Hannah traveled to Shiloh with a very costly sacrifice, worshiped God, and left Samuel in the care of Eli the High Priest. Hannah kept her promise to God. "For this child I prayed, and the Lord has granted me my petition which I asked of Him. Therefore I also have lent him to the Lord; as long as he lives he shall be lent to the Lord," (vv. 27-28).

Hannah's faith is expressed in her faithfulness. She kept her word, even when it cost her dearly. Imagine how much faith it took for this mother to pray fervently to have a child, and then, after finally receiving a son, to give him away to God's service. She did not completely walk out of her son's life. She visited him every year and continued to care for him as best she could (1 Sam. 2:18-19), but she no longer had him in her arms and cared for him as a mother loves to do.

> **NAZARITE VOW**
>
> Hannah's vow to God included the language of a Nazarite vow: "and no razor shall come upon his head." The Nazarite vow is discussed in detail in Numbers 6:1-21. A Nazarite vow was a time of consecration; a time in which one separated himself to God for a special reason and for a specific time. There are only three men mentioned in the Bible who were under a Nazarite vow for life: Samson, Samuel, and John the Baptist.

9. Describe the sacrifice Hannah had to make in order to keep her vow. _____
   _____
   _____
   _____

10. How did God reward this sacrifice (1 Sam. 2:20-21)? _____
    _____
    _____
    _____

11. Explain the significance of Samuel's name (1 Sam. 1:20). _____
    _____
    _____
    _____

Our Faithfulness

Just like Hannah, our faith is expressed in our faithfulness. God takes our word very seriously.

Under the Law of Moses, a vow was considered a sacred and binding promise. It had to be kept (Deut. 23:21-23; Ps. 66:13-14; Eccl. 5:4-5).

In the New Testament, the Lord condemned the scribes and the Pharisees for finding ways to get out of keeping their word. Both Jesus and James tell us to be people of our word (Matt. 5:33-37; James 5:12).

Faithfulness must be a trait that characterizes every Christian. It is a fruit of the Spirit (Gal. 5:22-23). As we follow the teaching of the Holy Spirit, found in the word of God, we discover how important it is to be trustworthy—to be people of our word.

While we do not make vows like those found in the Old Testament, there are two important promises that we will likely make to God in our lifetime. The first is our decision to become a Christian. When we obey the gospel, we are entering into a covenant with God, promising to be faithful to Him for the rest of our lives. God, in turn, promises to grant us a home in Heaven if we will remain faithful. We trust God to keep His word (2 Tim. 1:12), but God expects us to keep our promise to Him. Second, when we get married we are entering into a covenant made with God and our spouse in which we promise to honor our marriage bond until it is broken by death (Rom. 7:2-3). If we divorce our spouse for any reason other than fornication (Matt. 19:9), we are breaking a promise that God expects us to keep.

12. What did God expect people to do with regard to the vows they made (Deut. 23:21-23; Eccl. 5:4-5)? _____
_____
_____

13. Describe how becoming a Christian and getting married are two promises God expects us to keep. _____
_____
_____

14. Is it important to keep your word? Why? _____

    _____

    _____

15. What reaction will people likely have when they know you do not keep your word? _____

    _____

    _____

Conclusion

The name Hannah means *a woman of grace*. Because of her faith in God she was able to handle her adversity in a graceful manner. She did not create problems in her family by striking back at Peninnah or blaming her husband. She did not stop worshiping God. She quietly took the matter to God in prayer.

God answered her prayer and granted her request. Hannah was faithful to her promise and kept her word. God expects us to be people of our word. Those who "walk by faith" will do their best to keep their promises.

Lesson 6

DAVID
Faith To Face A Giant

The phrase "David vs. Goliath" has come to stand for any mismatch in which the underdog takes an unexpected victory. The story of the little shepherd boy defeating the giant was one of the first steps taken by David in becoming the greatest king in the history of Israel. It has inspired many people, but it is more than a mere story. This event actually occurred.

This Bible account is important to us because we all face giants in our walk of faith. Our "giants" take many different forms. Anything that causes a paralyzing fear in the life of a Christian is a "giant." Perhaps our "giant" is a person who is giving us a hard time for being a Christian. Perhaps it is a difficult decision we are facing. Perhaps it is a bad habit that we can't seem to break. We all face giants in our life, and this is one area in which our faith helps us.

First, we are going to look at the threat posed by Goliath. Second, we are going to contrast the reaction of Saul and his army with that of David. Third, we are going to learn how faith gives us courage to face and defeat our "giants."

> Moved with indignation and courage, David expressed his faith in God's power to deliver and won the victory.

Goliath

The army of the Philistines was encamped against the army of Israel. Each army had won victories in this on-again off-again war, but this time the Philistines seemed to have an advantage—a champion named "Goliath."

The Bible describes Goliath as a very intimidating foe (1 Sam. 17:4-7). He stood over nine and a half feet tall. The total weight of his bronze armor was between 125-200 pounds. The head of his spear weighed between 21-25 pounds. Try to imagine standing in front of this man!

Goliath stepped forward and spoke to the army of Israel. Instead of both armies fighting and losing casualties, he challenged Israel to produce one man who would fight with him to the death. The result of this fight would decide who won the battle between the armies (vv. 8-9).

Confident of his ability to defeat any Israelite, Goliath went on to say, "I defy the armies of Israel this day; give me a man, that we may fight together" (v. 10). Goliath was taunting and insulting the army of Israel, but he was also speaking against the God of Israel.

This scare tactic worked. The men of Israel looked upon Goliath and saw an impossible obstacle. "When Saul and all Israel heard these words of the Philistine, they were dismayed and greatly afraid" (v. 11, see v. 24). Goliath approached the army of Israel with this challenge twice a day for forty days (v. 16). This threat was not going away! However, the army of Israel was paralyzed by fear. No man dared to take him up on his challenge.

1. Describe the appearance of Goliath (1 Sam. 17:4-7). _____
   _____
   _____

2. What challenge did Goliath make to the army of Israel (vv. 8-9)? _____
   _____
   _____
   _____

3. How did the Israelites react to Goliath (vv. 11, 24)? _____
   _____
   _____

4. In ridiculing the army of Israel, who was Goliath really speaking against? ___
_____

David's Indignation

David was too young to be enlisted in Saul's army. His three oldest brothers were at the battle, but David was home tending his father's sheep.

David's father sent him to the battlefront with supplies for his brothers. While he was there, he saw Goliath and heard his taunting challenge (1 Sam. 17:20-23). The giant caused the men of Israel to draw back in fear (v. 24), but it brought forth a different emotion in David.

"Then David spoke to the men who stood by him, saying, 'What shall be done for the man who kills this Philistine and takes away the reproach from Israel? For who is this uncircumcised Philistine, that he should defy the armies of the living God?'" (v. 26).

Walking by faith gives one an entirely different perspective. The men of Israel saw a well-armed and well-trained giant. Israel was motivated by Goliath's size, but something else motivated David.

Unlike Saul and the rest of the Israelites, David did not look upon Goliath as an opponent too big to overcome, but as a target too big to miss. David saw an arrogant blasphemer who dared to defy the army of the living God! In referring to Goliath as "uncircumcised," David was making reference to the fact that Goliath was not a part of God's covenant people. He was without God's protection. His size did not matter! He could be defeated!

David also expressed his disappointment that none of the Israelites had taken Goliath up on his challenge. When his own brother tried to silence him, David asked, "Is there not a cause?" (vv. 28-29). Indeed, there was a cause worth fighting. God had been blasphemed. The army of the God of Israel had been reproached. This reproach needed to be taken away by killing Goliath. Why wasn't someone doing something?

Today, the enemies of God can be very intimidating. The teacher who presents Evolution as a fact appears to have scientific facts on his side. The atheist who ridicules believers appears to have good arguments against the existence of God. Worldly people who put down those who live by the Bible's standard of morality seem to be in the majority. However, when we look through our eyes of faith, we see that none of these arguments or individuals are any match against our God.

5. How did David react to Goliath's challenge (1 Sam. 17:26)? _____

_____

_____

_____

6. What did David mean when he called Goliath "uncircumcised"? _____

_____

_____

_____

7. According to David, there was a "cause" worth fighting for (v. 29). What was this cause? _____

_____

_____

David's Courage

The words spoken by David soon spread throughout the camp and came to the attention of King Saul. When David was brought before the king, he said, "Let no man's heart fail because of him; your servant will go and fight with this Philistine" (1 Sam. 17:32). Saul protested David's offer, stating he was no match for this well-trained soldier, but David did not agree.

David had confidence to face Goliath. While Goliath's confidence came from his size, his training and his armor, David's confidence came from his faith. David answered Saul by talking about his challenges as a shepherd (vv. 34-36). When a lion, and later a bear, had come and taken one of the lambs out of the flock, David had chased after it, saved the lamb from its mouth and then killed the predator.

David went on to assure Saul: "The Lord, who delivered me from the paw of the lion and from the paw of the bear, He will deliver me from the hand of this Philistine" (v. 37). David's faith in God was based upon what God had done for him in the past. Our faith is based upon the word of God (Rom. 10:17). In the Bible, God has established a track record of helping His people face and overcome their fears and their foes. As we read and study the Bible, our faith in God's willingness to help us becomes stronger. "For whatever things were written before were written for our learning, that we through the patience and comfort of the Scriptures might have hope," (Rom. 15:4).

8. From what wild beasts had God delivered David (1 Sam. 17:37)? _____
_____
_____

9. Explain why this gave David confidence to face Goliath. _____
_____
_____

10. Where does our faith come from (Rom. 10:17)? _____
_____
_____

11. How does faith and knowledge of God's word help us become stronger? __
_____
_____
_____

David's Victory

Saul tried to outfit David with his armor, but he couldn't walk in it. Instead he chose five smooth stones, took his sling, and stepped out onto the battlefield to accept Goliath's challenge (1 Sam. 17:38-40).

Goliath finally had a challenger. He drew near expecting to see a soldier, but he saw a shepherd boy. He ridiculed David and said, "Come to me, and I will give your flesh to the birds of the air and the beasts of the field!" (v. 44).

David was not intimidated by this unbeliever. He was confident in his victory. "You come to me with a sword, with a spear, and with a javelin. But I come to you in the name of the Lord of hosts, the God of the armies of Israel, whom you have defied. This day the Lord will deliver you into my hand, and I will strike you and take your head from you. And this day I will give the carcasses of the camp of the Philistines to the birds of the air and the wild beasts of the earth, that all the earth may know that there is a God in Israel. Then all this assembly shall know that the Lord does not save with sword and spear; for the battle is the Lord's, and He will give you into our hands," (vv. 45-47).

Notice the reason David faced Goliath. It was not because Goliath had insulted or sinned against David. It was because Goliath had insulted and sinned against God. This victory was to send a message. In defeating the giant without any military weapon in his hand, the men of Israel would learn that God protects them by His own strength, and the world would know that the God of Israel was the true and living God.

We send the same message when we walk by faith today. If we allow the pressures of this world to intimidate us, and we draw back and hide our faith in fear, Satan wins the victory. However, if we let our light shine in this world, even in moments when our faith is challenged the most, others see our good works and glorify our Father in heaven (Matt. 5:16).

David ran to Goliath, placed a stone in his sling and struck the giant between the eyes. He fell on his face. Not having a sword of his own, David drew Goliath's own sword, killed him and cut off his head. The Philistines fled and Israel pursued them (1 Sam. 17:48-54).

12. What weapons did David take with him when he faced Goliath (1 Sam. 17:40)?

_____

_____

13. What message did David intend to send by defeating Goliath (vv. 46-47)? ___

_____

_____

14. Explain how we can help other Christians by standing for the truth. _____

_____

_____

_____

15. Explain how we can help non-Christians by standing for the truth. _____

_____

_____

_____

Conclusion

Both fear and faith are contagious. The Israelites were terrified of Goliath. Every day it seemed their fear grew worse and worse. Not even the king's generous reward could embolden one of them to step forward and accept the giant's challenge (1 Sam. 17:25). All these men saw was a giant who couldn't be beaten.

David saw an unbeliever who dared to defy and insult the name of God. Moved with indignation and courage, David expressed his faith in God's power to deliver, defeated Goliath and won the victory. His faith quickly spread throughout the army as they took their weapons and pursued the Philistines.

Which do you have—fear or faith? Are you like the Israelites, or are you like David? God has given us what we need. If we will walk by faith, we will be able to face and overcome our giants.

Lesson 7

JOSIAH
A Faith That Overcomes Poor Role Models

We learn the most from those whom we are the closest. While we have the ability to choose our friends and thus surround ourselves with good influences, we do not have the ability to choose our family members.

Sadly, sometimes one's role models are not the best examples to follow. Their example and influence can hinder us from being the kind of person God wants us to be. They influence us to develop poor attitudes, habits, and standards by which we make our decisions. Sometimes it is up to us to "break the cycle" that has existed in our families for generations. That is a lot to ask of a young person.

The presence of poor role models does not excuse a young person from becoming the kind of man or woman God wants them to be. Poor role models are an unfortunate hurdle that some young people have to face. While it is difficult, the bad influence of poor role models can be overcome. There are a number of young people in the Bible who overcame adverse circumstances in their life and served the Lord faithfully. One such person is young king Josiah.

> As a young king, Josiah overcame adverse circumstances in his life and served the Lord faithfully.

1. In your own words, describe what a "role model" is.

   _____
   _____
   _____

2. Using the following verses, explain why it is important to choose our companions wisely.
   a. Proverbs 13:20 - _____

   _____

   b. Proverbs 27:17 - _____

   _____

   c. 1 Corinthians 15:33 - _____

   _____

Josiah's Poor Role Models

King Josiah's family tree was not impressive. His grandfather, Manasseh, was an evil king (2 Chron. 33:1-9). He rejected the faithfulness of his father, good king Hezekiah, and followed after the sinful practices of the nations around Judah. He rebuilt the places of idol worship that his father had removed. He went so far as to erect altars dedicated to the worship of idols in the temple of God. Following the debased pagan practices of his day, Manasseh had some of his sons put to death in the name of an idol. He practiced soothsaying and consulted mediums. Of his reign, the Bible says, "He did much evil in the sight of the Lord, to provoke Him to anger…So Manasseh seduced Judah and the inhabitants of Jerusalem to do more evil than the nations whom the Lord had destroyed before the children of Israel" (vv. 6, 9).

Josiah's father, Amon, was even worse than Manasseh (2 Chron. 33:21-25). He was such a terrible king that he was killed by his own servants after reigning only two years.

3. How did Manasseh disrespect God's temple (2 Chron. 33:4-5, 7-8)? _____

_____

_____

4. What is meant when the Bible tells us Manasseh "caused his sons to pass through the fire in the Valley of the Son of Hinnom" (v. 6)? You may want to

consult a Bible Encyclopedia or other resource in finding your answer. _____

_____

_____

5. How bad had Judah become under Manasseh's reign (v. 9)? _____

_____

_____

_____

6. What kind of a king was Amon in comparison to Manasseh? _____

_____

_____

7. List the "bad behavior" seen in some of the worldly role models today. _____

_____

_____

_____

Josiah Broke the Cycle

Josiah became king when he was eight years old (2 Chron. 34:1). Despite his youth, his heritage (the unfaithfulness of his father and grandfather), and the manner in which he became king (his father's murder), the Bible identifies Josiah as a king who "did what was right in the sight of the Lord" (v. 2).

In the twelfth year of his reign, when he was twenty years old, he began to cleanse the entire nation of all practices of idolatry. He not only removed the pagan altars; he had them broken into pieces! He beat the idols and altars into dust then scattered it on the graves of those who had sacrificed upon them. He executed the priests who officiated at these pagan altars and desecrated the places of idol worship so no man could ever worship there again (vv. 4-5; 2 Kings 23:20).

After cleansing the nation of idolatry, he turned his attention to repairing the Temple (2 Chron. 34:8). As the Temple was being repaired, the workers discovered a copy of "the Book of the Law of the Lord given by Moses" (v. 14). This book had become lost in the Temple through years of neglect. When the book was read, Josiah led the nation in repentance and caused the entire nation of Judah to renew their covenant with God (vv. 14-33).

Josiah also led the nation in the observance of the Passover. Of this observance, the Bible says, "There had been no Passover kept in Israel like that since the days of Samuel the prophet; and none of the kings of Israel had kept such a Passover as Josiah kept..." (2 Chron. 35:18).

It would have been easy for this young king to have carried on with things just like his grandfather and father had done. Instead, he made real changes in the religious practices of the nation. He broke the cycle of sin and idolatry.

8. How old was Josiah when he began his reforms (2 Chron. 34:3)? _____ How did Josiah break the cycle? _____
_____
_____

9. Describe how Josiah's reforms were different from Hezekiah's reforms. ____
_____
_____
_____

10. What was found in the Temple (v. 14)? Why was it lost? _____
_____
_____
_____

11. How did Josiah react to the reading of the book (vv. 19-21)? Why? _____
_____
_____
_____

12. What did Josiah consult as he led the nation in observing the Passover (2 Chron. 35:4, 6, 12-13, 15)? _____

How Josiah Overcame His Poor Role Models

Josiah overcame his poor role models by making the decision to seek the Lord in his youth. He did not wait to "grow up" before learning what God expected of him. "For in the eighth year of his reign, while he was still young, he began to seek the God of his father David..." (2 Chron. 34:3).

Also, notice how Josiah sought the Lord by doing what was right in the sight of the Lord (v. 2). Like other men and women of faith, Josiah's faith was expressed in actions; in works of obedience. His actions were governed by what pleased God, not by what pleased his peers, his parents, or himself. He sought to discover what pleased the Lord, and then he lived his life by that standard.

The Bible encourages us to seek the Lord in our youth. "Remember now your Creator in the days of your youth, before the difficult days come, and the years draw near when you say, 'I have no pleasure in them,'" (Eccl. 12:1). Seeking the Lord in our youth helps us establish godly habits and avoid mistakes which can have lasting and haunting consequences.

13. What did Josiah do in the eighth year of his reign (2 Chron. 34:3)? _____

14. What advantages are there to seeking the Lord in one's youth? _____

15. How did Josiah manifest his faith in God (2 Chron. 34:2)? _____
_____
_____
_____

16. List some ways to be a good role model for others. _____
_____
_____
_____

Conclusion

Not everyone is blessed to be surrounded by good influences. While some young people have godly parents who are good Christians, others have parents who are not good role models. It is difficult to go against the examples and expectations of one's role models, but, with a strong faith in God, it can be done.

It is easy to blame our sinful decisions on the poor examples that surround us. However, true character is shown in a willingness to rise above our circumstances, break ungodly cycles, and live a life patterned after God's righteousness. Doing so will be difficult, but it will certainly please God, and it will allow us to become good role models for others to follow (Php. 3:17).

Lesson 8

SHADRACH, MESHACH, AND ABEDNEGO
Faith In The Face Of Fire

The book of Daniel provides encouraging accounts of young men passing incredible tests of faith. Not only was Daniel put to the test, but so were his three friends—Shadrach, Meshach, and Abednego. Like Daniel, these young men were taken from Judah into Babylonian captivity, trained to serve before the king, and became the king's most trusted advisors (1:20). Others became jealous of them and plotted their downfall.

Young people are called upon to face trails. There are times when their faith will be put to the test. This account is recorded to help young people see they are important to God and can do great things for God because of their faith.

Their Trial

In his pride, Nebuchadnezzar made a gold statue that was 90 feet tall and 9 feet wide (this is about two-thirds the size of the Statue of Liberty). He commanded all men to bow down and worship the statue. Any who refused to do so would be "cast immediately into the midst of a burning fiery furnace." When the music began to play, the people fell down and worshiped the gold statue (Dan. 3:1-7).

Some Chaldeans came and told Nebuchadnezzar that Shadrach, Meshach, and Abednego failed to regard the

Young people matter to God. Because you matter to God, your faith will be tested. You need to learn from the example of Shadrach, Meshach, and Abednego.

king and bow down to the image. The king was furious and told the three young men that if they were ready to fall down and worship the image that it would be good, but if not, they would be cast immediately into the fiery furnace. The king further intimidated them by asking "And who is the god who will deliver you from my hands?" (vv. 8-15).

The nature of their trial. These young men had an important decision to make. It was literally a matter of life and death to them. If they would bow down before the statue they would keep both their positions in the king's government (v. 12) as well as their lives. However, in doing so, they would be violating their conscience and disobeying God.

We may not be forced to bow down before golden statues, but young Christians are often pressured to make compromises regarding their faith. It is at these times when our faith is tested. Will we pass the test?

1. Explain the penalty for failing to worship the gold image (Dan. 3:6). _____

2. Why was it wrong for Shadrach, Meshach, and Abednego to bow down before the gold image (Ex. 20:4-5)? _____

3. What intimidating question did the king ask (Dan. 3:15? _____

4. In your own words, describe the dilemma faced by Shadrach, Meshach, and Abednego. _____

5. What did Jesus have to say about such a dilemma (Matt. 10:28)? _____

_____

_____

_____

6. Young Christians are pressured to make all kinds of compromises regarding their faith. Think for a moment and describe at least three of these compromises. _____

_____

_____

_____

Their Testimony

We learn a lot about the faith of these young men by the response they gave to the king.

They demonstrated faith in the power of God (vv. 16-17). The king had asked which god could save them. They felt no need to speak in defense of God, but boldly stated that God was able to deliver them from the fiery furnace and would deliver them from the king's hand. Imagine the boldness of making such a statement under these circumstances. Such boldness comes from great faith. However, their faith was shown to be even greater with their next statement.

They demonstrated faith in the will of God (v. 18). Even if it wasn't God's will to deliver them, they would never become unfaithful to God. Their faith in God was not dependent upon God's willingness to deliver them. Their faith in God was based upon the greatness of God. They did not serve God because God had promised to deliver them. They served God because He was God.

Notice their faith is expressed with a simple response—"No." Sometimes remaining faithful to the Lord is as simple as saying "no" to those who challenge us to sin.

7. Who did Shadrach, Meshach, and Abednego say could save them (Dan. 3:17)?
   _____
   _____

8. What price were they willing to pay in order to keep from bowing down before the gold image (Dan. 3:18)? _____
   _____
   _____

9. Why did Shadrach, Meshach, and Abednego serve God? _____
   _____
   _____
   _____

Their Triumph

The faith of these young men was rewarded in a remarkable expression of God's mercy and power (vv. 19-25). The three men were bound and thrown into the furnace. Because of the king's anger, the fire was made so hot that it killed the mighty men who threw them into the furnace. However, the three men were safe. The king learned that God was both willing and able to deliver His servants from the fiery furnace.

However, there is more to consider than the fact that God spared their lives. With every trial of faith comes a blessing. Sometimes these blessings are hard to see because we are so focused upon our trials, but they are always present. Consider the blessings gained by Shadrach, Meshach, and Abednego.

A new sense of freedom (vv. 23-25). They entered bound, but they were seen loose and walking around. The very thing that was intended to destroy them enabled them to walk freely. If endured with faith, our own trials can cause us to grow and mature to the point that we are free from things that "bind" us, like worry, stress, and doubt (James 1:2-4).

A new source of fellowship (v. 25). There was a fourth person in the fire. We are not sure who this fourth person was. It was likely an angel, but some have suggested it was Christ. Whoever it was, the presence of the fourth individual represents a closer fellowship with God. Facing trials can often draw us closer to God. It is at such times we see our need for God in a way we never saw it.

A new person praising God (vv. 26-28). The king and all his companions saw the three men survive the furnace. They saw that the fire had not affected their bodies, their hair, or even their clothes. This was no "freak of nature." It was divine protection! The king blessed God. Even though some will pressure us into compromising our faith, and ridicule us for choosing to remain faithful, others, who see our faithfulness will be drawn closer to God. It is a blessing to know we have helped others come to Christ.

A new opportunity for service (v. 30). The king promoted Shadrach, Meshach, and Abednego to higher positions in his kingdom. While we are not promised any secular promotions, our faithfulness gives us a good reputation and increased opportunities to serve God.

10. How did God deliver Shadrach, Meshach, and Abednego? Provide some details of this miracle. _____
_____
_____

11. How did the king react to this deliverance? Specifically, what did he say about God (Dan. 3:26, 28)? _____
_____
_____
_____

12. Identify some benefits received from having our faith tested? _____
_____
_____
_____

13. What did Shadrach, Meshach, and Abednego do with their bodies (Dan. 3:28)?
_____

14. What are we to do with our bodies (Rom. 12:1)? _____

Conclusion

This was not the only time one's faith was tested by fire. The apostle Peter spoke of a Christian suffering in this way: "In this you greatly rejoice, though now for a little while, if need be, you have been grieved by various trials, that the genuineness of your faith, being much more precious than gold that perishes, though it is *tested by fire*, may be found to praise, honor, and glory at the revelation of Jesus Christ" (1 Peter 1:6-7, emphasis mine - HR).

Young people matter to God. Because you matter to God, your faith will be tested. Learn from the example of Shadrach, Meshach, and Abednego. Stand strong in the face of opposition, remain faithful, and enjoy the blessings that come as a result.

Lesson 9

NEHEMIAH
The Faith To Build

Nehemiah was a Jew who lived during the time of the return from Babylonian captivity. It had been almost one hundred years since Zerubbabel had led the first wave of Jews back to Jerusalem. In that time, the Jews had managed to rebuild the Temple, but the walls protecting the city were still in ruins.

The walls were important in ancient cities. Walls gave a city protection from their enemies and gave the citizens a sense of strength, security and honor. Without its walls, the people of Jerusalem were "in great distress and reproach" (Neh. 1:3).

Nehemiah served as a cupbearer for Artaxerxes, the king of Persia (1:11). This was a very honorable position which gave Nehemiah very close access to the king. When Nehemiah learned of the condition of Jerusalem, he asked the king for permission to travel to the city and rebuild its walls.

The book of Nehemiah reads differently than any other book in the Bible. It reads like a journal in which Nehemiah chronicles his efforts to rebuild the walls of Jerusalem. It is in this unique book that we gain insight into how a man of faith takes on the task of rebuilding.

> Nehemiah prayed, planned, got personally involved, and persisted until the job was finished.

Nehemiah Prayed

Prayer is an important subject in the book of Nehemiah. Nehemiah mentions his prayers twelve different times throughout the book. It is interesting to note, not only what he says in his prayers, but especially the occasions which bring forth his prayers. This book gives us a great lesson on the role of prayer in our lives for us to be effective servants of God.

Nehemiah's first prayer was upon hearing of Jerusalem's reproach (Neh. 1:5-11). In this prayer, he acknowledged the unfaithfulness of his people, and God's righteousness in allowing them to be taken into captivity. However, he also appealed to God's faithfulness in keeping a promise to return His people to their land if they would repent. As the king's cupbearer, Nehemiah realized he was in a unique position to personally ask the king for help. He prayed for God to use him as a means of securing the favor of the king.

Nehemiah's second prayer is a Biblical example of a "quick" prayer (2:4). These have been called "bullet prayers" or "arrow prayers." When he finally had the opportunity to ask for the king's help, Nehemiah offered a quick prayer and then presented his plan to the king (vv. 5-8). These "quick" prayers played an important role in Nehemiah's life, but they did not define his prayer life. These "quick" prayers worked because Nehemiah was already spending "quality time" with God in prayer.

Nehemiah also relied upon prayer when he faced opposition in his work. When his enemies mocked and ridiculed his efforts, Nehemiah prayed (4:4-5). When they conspired against him, Nehemiah prayed (6:14). Nehemiah fought his battles with prayer.

1. Explain why fortified walls were important to ancient cities. _____
   _____
   _____

2. What was Nehemiah's occupation or position (Neh. 1:11)? Describe the job and its importance. _____
   _____
   _____

3. How many times does the book of Nehemiah mention his prayers? _____
   _____

4. Explain why the "quick" prayers were able to work for Nehemiah. _____
   _____
   _____
   _____

5. Examine your prayer life and list circumstances surrounding its need. _____
   _____
   _____
   _____

Nehemiah Planned

It takes planning to accomplish anything worthwhile. Nehemiah was able to rebuild the wall because he had a plan.

Nehemiah told the king that he was sad because Jerusalem, the city of his people, lied in ruins and its gates were burned with fire (Neh. 2:3). When the king asked what he wanted done about it, Nehemiah already had a well thought-out plan (vv. 5-8). When asked how long it would take, and when he would be back, Nehemiah already had an answer. Nehemiah also asked for letters from the king that would allow him to travel safely to Jerusalem and to take the timber needed to rebuild the wall.

When he arrived in Jerusalem, Nehemiah surveyed the walls and considered all the work that needed to be done (2:11-15). Then he presented his plan to rebuild the wall to the residents of Jerusalem (vv. 17-18). The details of this plan are carried out in chapter three. Nehemiah stationed specific people at specific sections of the wall and had all of them working together at the same time.

5. What two requests did Nehemiah make of the king (Neh. 1:7-8)? _____
   _____
   _____
   _____

6. What did Nehemiah do when he arrived in Jerusalem (2:13)? _____
   _____
   _____

7. Who built the section of the wall at the Sheep Gate (3:1)? _____
   _____
   _____

8. Several people made repairs to the wall in front of their own house (3:10, 23, 28-30). Explain how it was wise for Nehemiah to have these people work on the section of the wall near their own houses. _____
   _____
   _____

Nehemiah Personalized His Work

With just a short speech, Nehemiah motivated the Jews to start a task they had allowed to go undone for almost one hundred years. Notice what he said:

> Then I said to them, "You see the distress that *we* are in, how Jerusalem lies waste, and its gates are burned with fire. Come and let *us* build the wall of Jerusalem, that *we* may no longer be a reproach." And I told them of the hand of my God which had been good upon me, and also of the king's words that he had spoken to me. So they said, "Let *us* rise up and build." Then they set their hands to this good work (Neh. 2:17-18, emphasis mine – HR).

Nehemiah made this task personal. It was not about "their" reproach and what "they" needed to do. It was about what "we" needed to do. That made a great difference. The old adage is true, "People don't care what you know until they know that you care."

This was more than just a rallying cry. Nehemiah lived up to his words. He made personal sacrifices to be involved in the rebuilding of the wall.

- He was personally involved in the building project (4:21-23).
- His servants worked on the wall instead of serving him (4:16).
- He did not demand the governor's provisions. He did not lay heavy burdens upon the people as former governors had done, nor did he take advantage of the crisis by buying up land. He shared his provisions with others (5:14-19).

"The people had a mind to work" (4:6) because they finally had a leader who didn't mind working.

9. Describe how Nehemiah was able to motivate the people in his speech (Neh. 2:17-18). _____

_____

_____

10. Describe the personal sacrifices Nehemiah made to rebuild the wall:

   a. 4:16 – _____

   _____

   _____

   b. 4:21-23 – _____

   _____

   _____

   c. 5:14-19 – _____

   _____

   _____

11. Why didn't Nehemiah mistreat the people as other governors had done (5:15)?

_____

_____

_____

12. What personal sacrifices have I made for the work of the Lord and the church?

_____

_____

_____

Nehemiah Persisted In His Work

As a general rule, projects usually present more obstacles than are originally anticipated. While Nehemiah's plans made preparations for his safe travel and securing timber for the construction of the wall (Neh. 2:7-8), he did not realize there were other problems he would have to face. However, his faith in God allowed him to persist with his work in spite of these distractions.

Sanballat the Horonite and Tobiah the Ammonite proved to be a great thorn in his side as he rebuilt the wall. They tried to discourage the people by mocking their efforts to rebuild (4:1-3). Nehemiah took the matter to God in prayer and the people continued their efforts. Then Sanballat and Tobiah threatened to attack the city (vv. 7, 12). Nehemiah responded by setting guards to protect the workers and the work continued.

Realizing they could not intimidate the workers, these enemies directed their efforts towards Nehemiah himself. Sanballat and Geshem the Arab sent four messengers to Nehemiah asking him to come and meet them. He saw no reason for them to do this other than to do him harm, so he refused and continued with the work (6:1-4).

Next Sanballat sent an open letter which accused Nehemiah of planning to rebel against the king (vv. 5-9). Nehemiah knew exactly how to handle this problem. He knew it wasn't true, gave them a quick reply stating such, and continued his work.

Finally, these enemies tried to scare Nehemiah into a compromising situation, hoping to make him look like a coward before the people (vv. 10-13). Nehemiah refused to listen to this counsel and continued his work.

People of faith realize their walk will not be easy. We are instructed to "not grow weary while doing good" (Gal. 6:9) but to "be steadfast, immovable, always abounding in the work of the Lord, knowing that your labor is not in vain in the Lord" (1 Cor. 15:58). "The wall was finished" (Neh. 6:15) because Nehemiah persisted against opposition.

12. What efforts did Sanballat and Tobiah make to discourage the people from rebuilding the wall (Neh. 4:1-3, 7, 12)? _____

_____

_____

_____

13. How did Nehemiah respond to these efforts (4:4-5, 9, 13-14)? _____

_____

_____

_____

14. How did Nehemiah respond to the rumors that he was rebelling against the king (6:8-9)? _____

_____

_____

15. "And let us not grow _____ while doing _____, for in due season we shall reap if we do not _____ _____" (Gal. 6:9, NKJV).

Conclusion

Nehemiah had a job to do that no one else seemed interested in doing. Jerusalem was in reproach, and it desperately needed to be repaired. How was Nehemiah able to accomplish in 52 days what had been neglected for almost one hundred years? He *prayed, planned,* became *personally involved,* and *persisted* until the job was finished.

People of faith continue to do the same thing today. God may never call upon us to rebuild a wall around His city, but we must always be ready to labor in His kingdom to His glory.

Lesson 10

ESTHER
A Courageous Faith

Courage is a very honorable trait. This word has been defined as "the attitude of facing and dealing with anything recognized as dangerous, difficult, or painful" (Guralnik, 325). Courage can be described as the strength to take risks, face danger, endure difficulty, or withstand fear.

There is admiration for those around us who show great courage: the cancer patient who bravely battles their disease, the soldier who goes to war, the police officer who places his life in danger to help others, the firefighter who enters a burning building to rescue people, etc. All of these individuals exhibit great courage.

Courage is not something that comes naturally. It is a characteristic that has to be learned, often at an early age. For many of us, it took great courage to ride a bicycle without training wheels for the first time, to go to the dentist, to stand up to a bully, to take part in a school play, etc. We had fears regarding these types of situations, but we found strength to face them, and gained courage along the way.

Esther was a woman who was called upon to exhibit great courage. She put her life at risk to save both herself and the entire Jewish nation. Learning some things about this young woman and her unique challenge helps us see the connection between faith and courage.

> Esther's unique challange helps us see the connenction between faith and courage.

Esther

The story of Esther took place during the time of Israel's return from Babylonian Captivity. While Ezra and Nehemiah were doing their work in Jerusalem, most of the Jews were scattered throughout the Persian Empire. The book of Esther gives an account of a threat faced by these Jews and what one unlikely hero (Esther) did to save them from annihilation.

Esther was an orphan who was raised by her older cousin named Mordecai (Esther 2:5-8). Mordecai was a Jew who lived in Shushan, one of the capitals of the Persian Empire. He "sat within the king's gate" (v. 21), which means he was a royal officer in service to the king.

King Ahasuerus began to look for a queen. Beautiful young women were brought to him from all over the empire. Esther was brought to the king, but at Mordecai's urging, Esther did not reveal she was a Jew (vv. 8-10). Esther found favor in the sight of the king. He loved her and chose to make her his queen (vv. 17-18).

Afterwards, the king promoted one of his princes named Haman. All of the king's servants bowed and paid homage to Haman except Mordecai. This made Haman furious. In his wrath, he devised a plan to punish not only Mordecai, but all of the Jews. He tricked the king into authorizing a royal decree which commanded that, on a specified day, all the Jews were to be killed and their property plundered. This decree was sent throughout the entire Persian Empire (Esther 3). The Jews were doomed, for no decree of the king could be altered or revoked (1:19, 8:8).

1. Using your own words, provide a good definition for the word "courage." ___
   _____
   _____
   _____

2. Name someone you know who has shown courage in their life. How was their courage shown? _____
   _____
   _____

3. Who was Esther's cousin (Esther 2:7)? _____
    _____

4. What royal decree was passed because of the influence of Haman (Esther 3:13)? _____
    _____
    _____

5. In our country, laws can be changed and revoked. What unique feature existed regarding the decrees of the Persian kings (Esther 1:19, 8:8)? _____
    _____
    _____

Esther's Challenge

As the royal decree was spread across the 127 provinces of the Persian Empire, the Jews in every place mourned their fate by fasting and weeping in sackcloth and ashes. Even Mordecai expressed his sorrow by tearing his clothes, putting on sackcloth, and crying aloud in the city (Esther 4:1-3).

When Esther learned what Mordecai was doing, she sent new garments to him, but he would not accept them. Esther then sent one of her attendants to find out why Mordecai was in mourning. Mordecai sent back a copy of the royal decree calling for the extermination of all the Jews, along with a request that Esther go in to the king and intercede on behalf of her people (vv. 5-9).

Esther felt as if she could not fulfill this request. She told Mordecai, "All the king's servants and the people of the king's provinces know that any man or woman who goes into the inner court to the king, who has not been called, he has but one law: put all to death, except the one to whom the king holds out the golden scepter, that he may live. Yet I myself have not been called to go in to the king these thirty days" (v. 11).

Although they were married, the king and Esther did not enjoy a close relationship like husbands and wives do today. She hadn't seen him for thirty days, and wouldn't dare go in to see him unless she was called. To do so was to risk certain death. She sent word back to Mordecai hoping he would understand why she could not meet his request.

Mordecai did not accept Esther's excuse. He sent back word which shed more light on the urgency of the situation (vv. 13-14). Esther would not be safe just because she was in the king's palace. She would suffer the same fate as the rest of the Jews.

Mordecai also expressed his faith that God would deliver the Jews, but challenged Esther by saying, "Yet who knows whether you have come to the kingdom for such a time as this?" (v. 14).

Esther had no idea what Haman had done to her people. It seems she was the last Jew to learn of this plot. However, she has found herself thrown to the forefront of a crisis she would just as soon avoid.

6. Describe how the Jews responded to the royal decree calling for their destruction (Esther 4:1-3). _____

7. Mordecai asked Esther to go in to the king and plead on behalf of the Jews. Explain why Esther was afraid to do this (v. 11). _____

8. How did Mordecai express his faith in God (v. 14)? _____

9. How did Mordecai challenge Esther (v. 14)? _____

Esther's Courage

Esther accepted Mordecai's challenge. "Then Esther told them to reply to Mordecai: 'Go, gather all the Jews who are present in Shushan, and fast for me; neither eat nor drink for three days, night or day. My maids and I will fast likewise. And so I will go to the king, which is against the law; and if I perish, I perish!'" (Esther 4:15-16). She was willing to put her life in danger in order to save the Jews.

Courage is not the absence of fear. It is a willingness to face one's fears, to overcome one's fears, and to act in spite of one's fears. Courage is a choice. Notice some of the reasons Esther chose to act with courage.

Esther's Faith. Faith is intended to be our source of strength in overcoming our fears. "And this is the victory that has overcome the world - our faith" (1 John 5:4b).

When we walk by faith, we are able to look beyond the physical object causing our fear and see God's care and provision. "The Lord is my light and my salvation; whom shall I fear? The Lord is the strength of my life; of whom shall I be afraid?" (Ps. 27:1). "The Lord is on my side; I will not fear. What can man do to me?" (Ps. 118:6).

When we walk by faith, we remember the promise given to Joshua. "Have I not commanded you? Be strong and of good courage; do not be afraid, nor be dismayed, for the Lord your God is with you wherever you go" (Joshua 1:9).

When we walk by faith, we remember we are "more than conquerors through Him who loved us" (Rom. 8:37).

Esther's Mentor. Mordecai had taken care of Esther and given her good advice her entire life (Esther 2:7, 10, 20). This placed him in a position to have a great amount of influence with her. Perhaps no one else could have convinced Esther to put her life on the line, but when Mordecai expressed his faith, Esther found her faith (4:14-16).

It is good for us to surround ourselves with godly mentors and friends who will give us sound advice and strong encouragement (Prov. 13:20, 27:17).

Esther Looked Beyond Herself. In Esther's initial response to Mordecai, she was only thinking about herself. When she looked beyond herself and thought about the greater issue (saving her people), she found courage to speak boldly to the king. "Then Queen Esther answered and said, 'If I have found favor in your sight, O king, and if it pleases the king, let my life be given me at my petition, *and my people at my request.* For *we have been sold, my people and I,* to be destroyed, to be killed, and to be annihilated..." (Esther 7:3-4, emphasis mine, H.R.).

Although our faith is a very personal thing shared with God, faith must also motivate us to look outwardly upon other people. When we consider how others are involved and impacted by our decisions, we can find the courage to act in the face of our fears.

10. What is our victory over the world (1 John 5:4)? _____

_____

_____

11. What promise had God made to Joshua (Joshua 1:9)? _____

_____

_____

12. In your own words, explain what it means to be more than a conqueror. ___

_____

_____

_____

13. Explain how good friends and mentors can help us find courage. _____

_____

_____

_____

14. Who are some of your godly mentors? _____

_____

_____

15. How can considering the wellbeing of others help us find courage? _____

_____
_____
_____

Conclusion

Esther took courage and presented herself before the king. She found favor in his sight and he held out his scepter to her (Esther 5:2). At a banquet, she exposed the plot of Haman, and he was killed (Esther 7). However, the royal decree was still in effect and could not be revoked. Acting with Mordecai, Esther saw to it that another decree was written giving the Jews the right to protect themselves. Their lives were spared. To this day, Jews celebrate the feast of Purim as a remembrance of how Queen Esther delivered them from destruction.

Courage is a choice. There will be times in your life when you will have to face your fears and muster courage to overcome various challenges. Satan never allows our faith to go unchallenged. Developing a strong faith now prepares us for the times when we need to "be strong and courageous."

References

Guralnik, David B. *Webster's New World Dictionary of the American Language*. New York: Prentice Hall, 1986. Print.

Lesson 11

PETER
A Faith That Walks On Water

The miracle of Jesus walking on the water is recorded in three places: Matthew 14:22-33; Mark 6:45-52; and John 6:15-21. However, the record in Matthew is the only one that tells of Peter also walking on the water. This miracle gives some insight into the character of Peter and the struggles he faced in learning how to exercise his faith in the Lord.

Jesus put His disciples in a boat, sent them to the other side of the Sea of Galilee, and went up on the mountain alone to pray. When they reached the middle of the sea, a contrary wind arose and tossed the boat in the waves. Jesus saw them straining to row the boat (Mark 6:48). While they were struggling to keep the boat on course, Jesus came to them, calmly walking on the water.

Jesus came to them in the fourth watch of the night. The Romans divided the night into four watches: from six to nine in the evening, from nine to midnight, from midnight to three, and from three to six in the morning. This miracle took place sometime between 3:00-6:00 in the morning. The Lord had allowed the disciples to struggle on the sea for most of the night. This made the miracle more impressive, which made their faith stronger.

When the disciples saw Jesus walking on the water, they were troubled and cried out for fear (v. 26). Men do not walk on water. They thought they were seeing a ghost.

> The Lord taught His disciples they could do great things with the faith they possessed.

There are people today who believe in ghosts. Likewise, some Jews believed in ghosts. They believed the appearance of a ghost was an omen of impending evil. These men had been battling the storm all night. Now it seemed they were seeing a ghost. They cried out in fear, believing they were doomed.

Jesus acted quickly to relieve their fears. "Be of good cheer! It is I; do not be afraid" (v. 27). Why didn't they know who it was? It was dark and stormy. Possibly all they could see was the outline of a man.

Peter spoke first (v. 28). While the invitation to "be of good cheer" sounded inviting, Peter wanted some evidence that it really was Jesus. He told the Lord to command him to come to Him on the water.

Peter's Request

> And Peter answered Him and said, "Lord, if it is You, command me to come to You on the water." So He said, "Come." And when Peter had come down out of the boat, he walked on the water to go to Jesus (Matt. 14:28-29).

Peter wanted proof that it really was Jesus, so he posed a challenge. Jesus did not rebuke Peter for making this request. Instead, He invited Peter to join Him on the water. Our Lord's response to Peter's request teaches us some interesting things about the Lord.

Jesus welcomes our investigation. When Jesus said, "Come," He was giving Peter permission to step forth and see that it was Him. Jesus welcomes investigation from those who are sincerely seeking to learn if He is real (John 1:35-41). Today, we investigate and learn about Jesus by turning to His Word.

Jesus will never hinder us from developing greater faith. Peter needed to step out of the boat. He needed this experience. Jesus does not call upon us to defy the law of gravity and walk across a body of water, but He does call upon us to defy some things that seem logical to us. For instance, Jesus says we must love Him above all others, we must be willing to suffer for Christ and His cause, and we must be willing to lose our physical life in order to obtain eternal life (Matt. 10:37-39).

These are not always easy things to do, but our faith grows when it is challenged and exercised. Jesus never keeps us from strengthening our faith.

Jesus will never bid us to do something we cannot do. Logic would have told Peter to stay in the boat, but the Lord told him to walk out on the water and Peter did. We must have the same kind of faith that Peter had—a confident belief that we are able to do everything Jesus commands us to do (1 John 5:3). Indeed, we can do all things through Christ who strengthens us (Phil. 4:13).

- "For this is the love of God, that we _____ His commandments. And His commandments are not _____" (1 John 5:3).

1. Why did the disciples cry out in fear when they saw Jesus walking on the water (Matt. 14:26)? _____
   _____
   _____

2. Jesus welcomes our investigation. Explain how we can "investigate" Jesus today. _____
   _____
   _____

3. Identify some challenges Jesus sets before us in Matthew 10:37-39. _____
   _____
   _____
   _____

4. What does 1 John 5:3 say about the commandments of God? _____
   _____
   _____

5. From where does our faith come (Rom. 10:17)? _____
   _____
   _____

Peter's Problem

> But when he saw that the wind was boisterous, he was afraid; and beginning to sink he cried out, saying, "Lord, save me!" (Matt. 14:30).

As long as Peter was focused on Jesus, he remained on top of the water. When he took his eyes off of Jesus and looked at his surroundings, he became afraid and began to sink. The water did not overtake Peter and drag him under. Peter shifted his focus away from the source of his spiritual strength (the Lord) and began to be overwhelmed by his physical surroundings. His faith gave in to fear, fear created doubt, and he began to sink.

The same thing happens to us in our walk of faith. As long as we keep our "eyes" focused on Jesus, we will "remain afloat" (Heb. 12:2). Walking by faith (2 Cor. 5:7) means we walk with a strong spiritual focus. It does not mean we ignore physical realities. It means we view them in light of spiritual realities (1 John 4:4, 5:4).

Peter's Cry For Help

> ...he cried out, saying, "Lord, save me!" And immediately Jesus stretched out His hand and caught him... (Matt. 14:30-31).

Peter did the right thing when he began to sink. He did not try to handle it himself. He did not turn to his friends (They couldn't walk on water either!). He cried out to the Lord, and the Lord immediately stretched out His hand to save Peter.

We serve a sympathetic Lord who cares about us, understands our challenges, and helps us when we ask (Heb. 4:15-16). Jesus knows when we need to work through our problems to develop stronger faith, but He also knows when we can't do it alone and will help us through the storm.

- "Call upon Me in the day of _____; I will _____ you, and you shall glorify Me" (Psa. 50:15).

6. Explain why Peter began to sink (Matt. 14:30). _____

_____

_____

7. Upon whom are we to remain focused (Heb. 12:2)? _____

_____

_____

8. Can you think of a time when your focus upon your physical surroundings caused your faith to become weak? Describe what happened, and how you overcame this situation. _____

_____

_____

9. The Lord has promised to help us in our troubles. Explain what kind of High Priest Jesus is (Heb. 2:17-18, 4:15-16). _____

_____

_____

_____

Peter's Limitation

O you of little faith, why did you doubt? (Matt. 14:31).

Peter was walking on water! There was no reason he shouldn't have been able to continue doing so. The problem was not with the Lord's power and ability, but with Peter's faith. The Lord taught His disciples they could do great things with the faith they possessed.

"Then the disciples came to Jesus privately and said, 'Why could we not cast it out?' So Jesus said to them, 'Because of your unbelief; for assuredly, I say to you, if you have faith as a mustard seed, you will say to this mountain, "Move from here to there," and it will move; and nothing will be impossible for you'" (Matt. 17:19-20, cf. 21:21).

A mustard seed was the smallest of all seeds in Palestine. Jesus was not telling them they had to go and get more faith. He was telling them they could do great things when they used the faith they possessed, even if it was the smallest amount. Walking by faith does not mean we wait around until we have built up enough faith, it means we use the faith we have.

The Lord does not invite us to defy the laws of nature (to walk on water or move entire mountains), but He does require us to follow Him. There are great challenges along the strait and narrow path, but our faith helps us overcome these challenges.

10. According to Jesus, how much faith is needed to "move a mountain" (Matt. 17:20)? _____

_____

_____

11. Describe a time in your life when your faith helped you overcome a challenge or an obstacle. _____

_____

_____

_____

Conclusion

This miracle caused the disciples to worship Jesus and confess "Truly You are the Son of God" (v. 33). If we walk by faith, and keep our faith "afloat" during the storms of our life, others see and know our faith is real, helping them know that Jesus is truly the Son of God.

Do you have the kind of faith that will walk on water? How are you showing your faith?

MARTHA AND MARY
Making Priorities A Matter Of Faith

Martha and Mary lived with their brother Lazarus in the small village of Bethany. This village was located about two miles southeast of Jerusalem, on the other side of the Mount of Olives. These three siblings were dear friends of the Lord. "Now Jesus loved Martha and her sister and Lazarus" (John 11:5). It appears that Jesus was a familiar guest in their home. Although we aren't told specifically, Jesus likely stayed with them during the week before His crucifixion (Matt. 21:17).

While it is true that siblings are often alike in many ways, there are differences. The differences between Martha and Mary are brought to light in Luke 10:38-42. On this occasion, Martha invited Jesus and His companions into her home. While she busied herself in caring for her guests, Mary sat at Jesus' feet and listened to Him teach. Martha interrupted Jesus and requested that He tell Mary to help her. Our Lord's response to Martha teaches us how our faith should shape our priorities.

> We all have choices to make. What do our priorities say about our faith?

Martha's Problem

Luke tells us that Martha was "distracted with much serving" (Luke 10:40). Martha was busy, but she was not making up busy work for herself. In serving her guests, she was taking on a role that the customs of her culture would have expected her to fill. She was the one who welcomed Jesus and His companions into her home. Thus, she was obligated to care for them.

While we are not told exactly what Martha was preparing and serving her guests, we are told that she was doing "much serving." Formal meals in ancient Israel could consist of as many as three separate courses, along with a dessert. Martha was doing more than making sure her guests had food to eat, she was giving them the best she had to offer.

There was nothing wrong with Martha preparing and serving food to her guests, but Jesus said she was "worried and troubled about many things" (v. 41). She was fretting over the details; sweating the small stuff. The anxiety and stress she was feeling over her serving was "distracting" her from something important.

If we believe in God, we must believe He cares for us and will take care of us. Jesus is clear in teaching us that we are not to be worried over the physical things of this life (Matt. 6:25-33). Such worry is actually the result of a lack of faith: "O you of little faith" (v. 30). We are not to worry about our life (what we will eat, drink or wear) because we know God is aware of our needs (v. 32) and cares about us (v. 26). Our faith gives us freedom from being worried and troubled about many things.

1. How is Martha described in Luke 10:40? _____
   _____
   _____

2. Give some reasons we are not to worry about the physical things in our life (Matt. 6:25-26, 32). _____
   _____
   _____
   _____

3. Where does such worry come from (Matt. 6:30)? _____
   _____
   _____

4. In your own words, explain how a strong faith in God frees us from the need to worry. _____

_____

_____

Martha's Pride

Martha revealed something about herself in the statement she made to the Lord. She was struggling with her pride. "Lord, do You not care that *my* sister has left *me* to serve alone? Therefore tell her to help *me*" (Luke 10:40, emphasis mine, H.R.).

In ridiculing Mary in front of Jesus and the other guests, it never occurred to Martha that she was the one who was in the wrong. This is what pride does to us. It elevates our ego and our problems so high that it distorts our vision. We cannot see anyone's needs but our own, and we cannot see ourselves correctly.

Martha was busy serving others, which was a good work, but she was really focused on herself. This is an ugly episode in the life of an otherwise faithful and righteous woman.

People of faith are tempted by pride (1 John 2:16), but our faith helps us overcome our pride. Our faith allows us to see who we really are in the sight of God and our fellowman.

5. Use the following verses to identify some dangers associated with pride:

    a. Prov. 11:2 - _____

_____

    b. Prov. 13:10 - _____

_____

    c. Prov. 16:5 - _____

_____

d.　Prov. 16:18 - _____
　　　　_____

　　e.　Prov. 26:12 - _____
　　　　_____

　　f.　1 Peter 5:5 - _____
　　　　_____

6.　How are we to regard or esteem others (Phil. 2:3)? _____
_____
_____
_____

Martha's Priorities

Both Martha and Mary had a choice regarding how they would spend their time with Jesus in their home. Martha chose to give her attention to serving her guests. Mary chose to sit at Jesus' feet and listen to His teaching. According to Jesus, "Mary has chosen that good part" (Luke 10:42).

Jesus refused to tell Mary to help Martha because, in that situation, Mary had made the right choice. Mary was not being lazy or neglectful. She understood the true importance of that hour and that opportunity. She had her priorities straight. She valued the spiritual over the physical. It was not wrong for Martha to serve her guests, but the better choice would have been for her to take advantage of the opportunity to hear the word of God.

Not only must our faith be trained by the word of God to discern between good and evil (Heb. 5:12-14), but our faith must also help us distinguish between degrees. Sometimes the choices we have to make are not between good and evil or right and wrong. Sometimes it is a choice between what is better and what is best. People of faith strive to always make the best choices.

Christians aren't always distracted by worldly and sinful activities. We simply get busy and become sidetracked with the responsibilities and challenges of everyday life, leaving little or no time for the things that really matter—spiritual things. If we fail to make spiritual things a priority in our life, they will soon be neglected and left behind.

7. Use the following verses to identify some spiritual things which should be priorities in our life:

   a. Hebrews 10:25 - _____

   b. 1 Thessalonians 5:17 - _____

   c. Acts 17:11; Psalm 1:2 - _____

   d. 2 Corinthians 13:5 - _____

   e. Ephesians 6:11 - _____

   f. James 5:19-20 - _____

8. What happens if we fail to make spiritual things a priority in our life? _____
   _____
   _____
   _____

Mary's Blessing

"Mary of Bethany is seen three times in the Gospel record, and on each occasion, she is in the same place: at the feet of Jesus. She sat at his feet and listened to His Word (Luke 10:39), fell at His feet and shared her woe (John 11:32), and came to His feet and poured out her worship (John 12:3)" (Wiersbe, 213).

Jesus told Martha that "one thing is needed, and Mary has chosen that good part" (Luke 10:42). Mary had made spiritual things a priority. What Martha gave the Lord was service—food and shelter. What Mary gave the Lord was her attention and her heart.

This passage helps us understand that worship is to take priority over service. We need to be very careful of the things we allow to take us away from our worship and devotion to God. Sometimes families get busy and make compromises with their schedules. Homework, sports, or other activities may begin to replace Wednesday night Bible study. Sometimes the assemblies on the Lord's Day are missed so the family can go out of town for one reason or another. If this becomes a habit, any activity will be used as an excuse to miss services.

Mary had chosen the good part and it would not be taken away from her (v. 42). The hospitality Martha was providing was important, but it only provided a temporary benefit. Their stomachs would become empty and their bodies would become tired again. However, the bread of life given by Jesus on that occasion provided a spiritual blessing that would never pass away (1 Pet. 1:24-25).

- "And Jesus said to them, 'I am the _____ of life. He who comes to Me shall _____ hunger, and he who believes in Me shall _____ thirst'" (John 6:35).

9. Was Martha doing something unimportant or sinful in choosing to serve her guests? _____
_____

10. Was Mary being lazy or indifferent in choosing to sit at Jesus' feet and hear Him teach? _____
_____

11. Martha and Mary made different choices on this occasion. Explain why Mary had made a better choice. _____
_____
_____

12. Identify some things that can take us away from our worship and devotion to God. _____
_____
_____

13. Have you ever chosen an activity that took you away from your devotion to God? How did this make you feel? _____

_____

_____

14. Where are we to lay up our treasure (Matt. 6:19-20)? _____

_____

_____

Conclusion

Jesus gave Martha a mild rebuke, but notice what He rebuked: He did not criticize her desire to serve and care for her guests. Jesus rebuked Martha for her anxiety, her pride, and her misplaced priorities.

Instead of helping her sister serve their guests, Mary was found at Jesus' feet, listening to the word of God. According to Jesus, she had chosen the good part; the one thing that was needed.

This account gives us an opportunity to look at ourselves. We all have choices to make. What do our priorities say about our faith?

References

Wiersbe, Warren W. *The Bible Exposition Commentary, Vol. 1*. Colorado Springs, CO: Chariot Victor Publishing, 1989. 213. Print.

Lesson 13

JESUS CHRIST
A Faith That Gets Us Through A Crisis

The entire life of Jesus serves as an example for us to follow. There is one event in the life of our Lord in which He exhibited a great amount of faith in God and thus set an example for us. That is His prayer in the Garden of Gethsemane (Matt. 26:36-46).

Jesus did not have to suffer and die for our sins. It was something He chose to do. At the time of His arrest, He did not allow His disciples to fight for Him. He said, "Or do you think that I cannot now pray to My Father, and He will provide Me with more than twelve legions of angels?" (Matt. 26:53). Paul spoke of our Lord's voluntary death in the following manner: "And being found in appearance as a man, He humbled Himself and became obedient to the point of death, even the death of the cross" (Phil. 2:8).

Moments of suffering are times in which our faith is put to the test. The way our Lord conducted Himself in Gethsemane provides a great example of how our faith is to sustain us in our own trials and sufferings. Let's consider some lessons to be learned from Gethsemane.

> **Strong faith gives us the strength we need to be honest with our problems, face them, and see them through to the end.**

It Is OK To Give In To Natural Feelings

"And He took with Him Peter and the two sons of Zebedee, and He began to be sorrowful and deeply distressed" (Matt. 26:37).

Imagine what it must have been like for Peter, James, and John to see this happen. They had seen Jesus perform many powerful miracles, and had seen Him transfigured on the mountain (Matt. 17:1-2). Now they were seeing Jesus distressed and sorrowful. As a man, Jesus was coming to grips with the reality of His impending suffering and death.

Faith does not remove realities. Jesus teaches us that it is alright for us to give in to and experience human emotions. Some people try to hide their feelings and emotions, but the reality is that God has given us our emotions as a means of coping with and surviving extreme situations.

Tell Someone How You Feel

"Then He said to them, 'My soul is exceedingly sorrowful, even to death. Stay here and watch with Me'" (Matt. 26:38).

Jesus had a special relationship with these three disciples (Peter, James, and John). Jesus had helped them in their moments of weakness, now He needed their help. Jesus confided in them, telling them exactly how He was feeling. He asked them to stay with Him and watch with Him.

Some view asking for help as evidence of weakness and may try to reason, "My faith is strong enough to get me through this." But Jesus asked for help from His friends.

It is a good thing to seek help from our friends when we are suffering. They can pray for us (James 5:16) and help us bear our burdens (Gal. 6:2).

1. Was Jesus forced to suffer on the cross for our sins? Provide scripture to support your answer. _____
   _____
   _____

2. What change took place with Jesus in the Garden (Matt. 26:37)? _____
   _____
   _____

3. What request did Jesus make of Peter, James, and John (Matt. 26:38)? _____

_____

_____

4. What does Ecclesiastes 4:9-12 say about the benefits of having friends? ___

_____

_____

_____

It's Time To Pray

"He went a little farther and fell on His face, and prayed, saying, 'O My Father, if it is possible, let this cup pass from Me; nevertheless, not as I will, but as You will'" (Matt. 26:39). Jesus found the strength He needed to face the cross in prayer. That same strength is available for us as well (Phil. 4:6-7). In this passage, Jesus teaches that prayer is a time for us to cast our troubles upon the Lord (1 Pet. 5:7). It is a time for us to let God know what is troubling us, what we are facing, and how we feel about it.

Also, this passage teaches us that prayer is a time for us to accept the will of God. "Not as I will, but as You will." Our Lord's request was that He could be spared the pain and suffering of the cross. However, He was willing to accept the Lord's will in this situation.

Prayer is an exercise in faith. We are casting our cares upon a God who we cannot see. There are times when it takes a greater amount of faith to accept God's answer to our prayers, especially when God seems to be telling us "No!"

We Must Be Understanding of Others

"Then He came to the disciples and found them sleeping, and said to Peter, 'What! Could you not watch with Me one hour? Watch and pray, lest you enter into temptation. The spirit indeed is willing, but the flesh is weak'" (Matt. 26:40-41).

Jesus had asked His friends to watch with Him. When He returned to them He found them asleep. They had let Him down, but He did not chastise them. In fact, He acknowledged their struggles. He knew they meant well (the spirit was willing), but He also knew they were exhausted (the flesh is weak).

A strong faith allows us to remain patient and understanding of others while we are suffering. Some people only focus upon themselves, but faith causes us to look outward seeing the needs and weaknesses of others.

5. In your own words, explain why prayer is an exercise of faith. _____
   _____
   _____
   _____

6. What promise is available through prayer (Phil. 4:7)? _____
   _____
   _____

7. What was more important to Jesus: that His will be done or that God's will be done (Matt. 26:39)? _____
   _____

8. What did Jesus understand about Peter, James and John (Matt. 26:41)? ____
   _____
   _____

It's Time To Keep On Praying

"Again, a second time, He went away and prayed, saying, 'O My Father, if this cup cannot pass away from Me unless I drink it, Your will be done.' And He came and found them asleep again, for their eyes were heavy. So He left them, went away again, and prayed the third time, saying the same words" (Matt. 26:42-44).

Some people have the idea that we should only ask God something once, and that is enough. However, Jesus prayed three separate times in the Garden of

Gethsemane. Jesus taught us to be persistent in our prayers (Luke 18:1-8). In this parable, Jesus spoke of an unjust judge who granted a widow's request, not because she was right, but because she constantly asked him for help. If he was willing to grant her request, how much more will our loving Heavenly Father grant our requests unto Him?

It Is Time To Face Our Problems

"Then He came to His disciples and said to them, 'Are you still sleeping and resting? Behold, the hour is at hand, and the Son of Man is being betrayed into the hands of sinners. Rise, let us be going. See, My betrayer is at hand'" (Matt. 26:45-46).

When the time came for Jesus to face the cross, He did not try to run away. He went out to meet the mob that had come to arrest Him. Likewise, we cannot run away from our problems. They have to be faced sooner or later.

Some people are afraid of facing their problems. They do not want to deal with sorrows or tragedies. They run from them. Some go so far as to seek escape through drugs, alcohol, or even suicide. Strong faith gives us the strength we need to be honest with our problems, face them, and see them through to the end (2 Tim. 1:7).

9. How many times did Jesus pray in the Garden of Gethsemane? _____

10. How many times did Paul pray regarding his thorn in the flesh (2 Cor. 12:7-9)?

11. Explain some ways people try to run from their problems. _____

12. What has God given us to help us face our problems (Eph. 6:10-18)? _____
_____
_____
_____

Conclusion

While Jesus was fully God in the flesh, He faced the cross as a man, enduring every type of pain and agony that came with the cross using the same resources that are available to every one of us. The manner in which He endured the cross serves as a valuable example to us today. "For to this you were called, because Christ also suffered for us, leaving us an example, that you should follow His steps" (1 Peter 2:21).

When facing a trial, it is all right for us to feel emotions and rely upon friends. It is also important for us to lean upon God in prayer. However, we must face the trials that come upon us. We can do so, if we will walk by faith.

www.ingramcontent.com/pod-product-compliance
Lightning Source LLC
Chambersburg PA
CBHW070622050426
42450CB00011B/3107